PRAYERSCRIPTS
Speaking God's Word Back to Him

SCRIPTURES & PRAYERS FOR
ENGAGING
THE ENEMY

70 DAYS OF PRAYER TO REBUKE THE ENEMY AND RELEASE GOD'S POWER

CYRIL OPOKU

Scriptures & Prayers for Engaging the Enemy: 70 Days of Prayer to Rebuke the Enemy and Release God's Power

© 2025 Cyril Opoku. *PrayerScripts*. All rights reserved.

No part of this publication may be reproduced, stored in a retrieval system, or transmitted in any form or by any means—electronic, mechanical, photocopy, recording, or otherwise—without the prior written permission of the publisher, except in the case of brief quotations used in reviews, articles, or devotionals.

Published by *Quest Publications*

ISBN: 978-1-988439-58-7

Cover design by *Quest Publications (questpublications@outlook.com)*

Unless otherwise indicated, all Scripture quotations are taken from the World English Bible (WEB), which is in the public domain. For more information, visit: www.worldenglish.bible

This book is a work of devotional encouragement. It is not intended to replace biblical study, pastoral counsel, or professional therapy.

Printed in the United States of America.

First Edition: July 2016
Second Edition: July 2025

For more books like this, visit *PrayerScripts:* https://prayerscripts.org

Contents

Preface .... *vi*
How to Use This Devotional .... *vii*

PART 1: REBUKING THE ENEMY 1
Day 1:   The Lord Rebuke You 2
Day 2:   Stillness at His Voice 3
Day 3:   At Your Rebuke 4
Day 4:   Peace, Be Still 5
Day 5:   He Rebuked the Sea 6
Day 6:   Scatter the Beasts 7
Day 7:   Flee Like Chaff 8
Day 8:   He Rebuked the Unclean Spirit 9
Day 9:   The Great Vengeance 10
Day 10: With Fire and Sword 11
Day 11: One Shall Chase a Thousand 12

PART 2: RELEASING TERROR UPON THE ENEMY 13
Day 12: Terror Fell on Them 14
Day 13: Hearts Melted in Fear 16
Day 14: Dread and Awe 18
Day 15: Thundered Against the Enemy 19
Day 16: Terrors Overtake Them 20
Day 17: Driven to Darkness 21
Day 18: The Arrows of the Almighty 22
Day 19: Terrors Turn Upon Me 23
Day 20: The Sound of Dread 24
Day 21: The Sound of Panic 25
Day 22: Fear on Every Side 27

Day 23:	Sudden Destruction	29
Day 24:	The Bronze Drawn Sword	30
Day 25:	Terror Within and Without	31
Day 26:	He Shall Cut Down the Branches	32
Day 27:	The Fear of Judah	33
Day 28:	Great Fear Where None Was	34
Day 29:	Not Afraid by Night	35
Day 30:	Far from Oppression	36
Day 31:	Sanctify the Lord	37

PART 3: PRAYING FOR THE FALL OF THE ENEMY 38

Day 32:	Turned Back and Destroyed	39
Day 33:	We Rise and Stand Upright	40
Day 34:	Sure Downfall	41
Day 35:	They Went Backward and Fell	42
Day 36:	Satan Fell Like Lightning	43
Day 37:	When the Wicked Came	44
Day 38:	Let God Arise	45
Day 39:	Subdued Under My Feet	46
Day 40:	No One Shall Stand	47
Day 41:	Fallen Suddenly	48
Day 42:	Slippery Places	49
Day 43:	Chased by the Angel of the Lord	50
Day 44:	In Due Time	51
Day 45:	Slippery Darkness	52
Day 46:	Stumble in the Dark	53

PART 4: TREADING UPON THE ENEMY 54

Day 47:	Watch Me Rise	55
Day 48:	Power to Tread	56

Day 49:	Crushed Beneath His Feet	57
Day 50:	The Fall of the Lofty City	58
Day 51:	Do Valiantly	59
Day 52:	Under My Feet	60
Day 53:	None Like My God	61
Day 54:	Surefooted Victory	62
Day 55:	Feet on Their Necks	63
Day 56:	Sit at My Right Hand	64
Day 57:	Until All Enemies Fall	65
Day 58:	The Fall of the Proud	66
Day 59:	Treading the Lofty Down	67
Day 60:	Ashes Under My Feet	68
Day 61:	Like a Lion Among Flocks	69
Day 62:	Dust Beneath My Feet	70
Day 63:	War Horses of the Lord	71
Day 64:	The Winepress of Justice	72

PART 5: WHEN HEAVEN STRIKES 73

Day 65:	Who Can Stand?	74
Day 66:	They Shall Be as Nothing	75
Day 67:	Delivered from the Strong	76
Day 68:	Brought Down from the Heights	77
Day 69:	He Shall Prevail	78
Day 70:	Lightning and Deliverance	79

Epilogue *80*
Encourage Others with Your Story *81*
More from PrayerScripts *82*

Preface

Spiritual warfare is not a metaphor—it's a reality. Every believer is born into a battle, and though the victory has been won through Christ, the war still rages in our world, our minds, and our daily lives. *Scriptures & Prayers for Engaging the Enemy* was written for those who refuse to stay silent in the face of darkness. It is for the weary intercessor, the bold worshipper, the everyday believer who knows that passivity is no longer an option.

This devotional is not just about prayer—it's about positioning. It is about stepping into the authority given to us by Jesus, aligning our words with God's Word, and releasing prayers that shake the gates of hell. These 70 days are not random reflections—they are targeted strikes, rooted in Scripture, forged in spiritual truth, and saturated with the cry for justice, victory, and divine intervention.

Here, you will not find passive platitudes. You will find fire. You will find warfare. You will find the courage to stand, the strength to speak, and the faith to believe that your prayers matter—that heaven hears and hell trembles.

You were not made to be defeated. You were made to overcome. Let these pages help you rise.

Fighting His Battles,
Cyril O. (July 2025)

How to Use This Devotional

Scriptures & Prayers for Engaging the Enemy: 70 Days of Prayer to Rebuke the Enemy and Release God's Power is designed to equip and ignite you for 70 days of strategic, Scripture-based prayer. Each daily entry focuses on a single theme or Scripture, offering a title, passage reference, and a deeply personal prayer written in the first person.

Here's how to engage with it daily:

1. **Read the Scripture Passage** — Meditate on the verse or passage noted at the top of the entry. Read it slowly. Let it speak.
2. **Pray the Prayer Aloud** — Speak the prayer out loud, making it your own. Let your heart agree with the words as a declaration of faith and spiritual alignment.
3. **Pause and Reflect** — Sit with what God is revealing. You may wish to journal what you're hearing or experiencing in response.
4. **Stand in Agreement** — Consider praying these words over others—your family, your church, your city. Warfare is rarely private. Agreement multiplies impact.

You can journey through the devotional in order or jump to a section that speaks to your current battle. The five parts are arranged progressively—from rebuking the enemy to declaring God's violent intervention from heaven—so working through them in order will build momentum.

This is not just a devotional—it is a spiritual weapon. Use it daily. Use it boldly. Use it as one who stands with heaven's armies.

PART 1: Rebuking the Enemy

There are moments in spiritual battle when silence is not an option. When the enemy speaks lies, we answer with truth. When darkness advances, we respond with authority—not our own, but the authority given to us by the Lord Jesus Christ. To rebuke the enemy is not to argue, but to stand. It is to declare, by faith, that the God who speaks storms into stillness and casts out demons with a word is the same God who lives within us.

In this section, we align our prayers with the voice of Heaven. We call upon the Lord who rebukes the devourer, silences accusers, and scatters every wicked scheme. These prayers are not whispered in fear—they are spoken in holy boldness, rooted in Scripture, and carried by the authority of God's Word. Let your heart be stirred, your faith be strengthened, and your voice rise as you engage the enemy with the rebuke of the Lord.

Day 1: The Lord Rebuke You

> Yahweh said to Satan, "Yahweh rebuke you, Satan! Yes, Yahweh who has chosen Jerusalem rebuke you! Isn't this a burning stick plucked out of the fire?"
> —Zechariah 3:2 WEB

Lord, I stand before You, not in my own righteousness, but covered by Your mercy. The enemy has accused me, tried to stain me with shame, but You, O Lord, have spoken a better word. You have said, "The Lord rebuke thee, O Satan." And I cling to that declaration today.

I may feel like a brand plucked out of the fire—scarred, singed, and weak—but You have rescued me. You have pulled me from destruction and called me Your own. I am not abandoned to the flames. I am redeemed. I am chosen.

Father, I trust in Your rebuke against the adversary. I do not fight in my own strength, but I take shelter in Your authority. When the enemy whispers lies, You silence him with truth. When he brings up my past, You remind him that I have been cleansed. When he tries to pull me down, You lift me up with Your right hand.

Cover me today, Lord, with the garments of Your salvation. Clothe me in the righteousness that comes from Christ alone. Set Your seal upon me, that the enemy may know I am Yours and cannot be touched without Your permission.

Thank You for being my defender, my advocate, and the One who stands with me in the fire. I surrender my fears and rise in faith, trusting that every accusation falls powerless at the sound of Your voice.

In Jesus' name, Amen.

Day 2: Stillness at His Voice

> At your rebuke, God of Jacob, both chariot and horse are cast into a dead sleep.
> —Psalms 76:6 WEB

Mighty God, at the rebuke of Your voice, both the chariot and the horse are cast into a deep sleep. You, Lord, are the One who silences the strength of the enemy with a single breath. When the powers of darkness rage, You speak—and they are still. When I feel surrounded, You remind me that nothing moves without Your permission.

I rest in the confidence of Your power. I do not need to be afraid, for even the fiercest weapons of the enemy fall lifeless when You rise in defense of Your people. You are my shield and my stronghold. You speak, and every force that comes against me is disarmed.

So today, I stand under Your covering, rebuking every lie, every fear, every force that rises in opposition to the will of God for my life. I do not trust in horses or chariots—I trust in the name of the Lord my God. You alone are to be feared, for who can stand before You when once You are angry?

Let every scheme of the enemy be brought to nothing at the sound of Your command. I am safe in You. I walk forward, not in fear, but in faith, because You are the One who fights for me.

In Jesus' name, Amen.

Day 3: At Your Rebuke

> At your rebuke they fled. At the voice of your thunder they hurried away.
> —Psalms 104:7 WEB

At Your rebuke, O Lord, the waters fled; at the voice of Your thunder, they hurried away. So today, I lift my heart to You, knowing that the same power that parted the seas and drove back the floods still moves on my behalf.

When chaos rises around me—when fear, confusion, or attack threatens to overwhelm—You speak, and everything must bow. At Your word, disorder retreats. At Your command, what once seemed unstoppable is turned back. You are the God who commands the waters, and You command the enemy with the same authority.

Lord, I rest in the shelter of Your voice. I do not tremble at the waves of trouble, for You are greater. I do not fear the flood, for You can rebuke it in an instant. Let every spiritual assault melt away at the sound of Your thunder. Let every plan formed against me scatter in haste.

Rebuke the devourer, silence the accuser, and drive out the darkness that seeks to cloud my soul. I hide myself in Your presence, where peace flows like a river and nothing can touch me without passing through Your hand.

Thank You, Lord, that Your voice still speaks and still delivers. I trust in the power of Your word and take refuge in Your strength.

In Jesus' name, Amen.

Day 4: Peace, Be Still

> He awoke, and rebuked the wind, and said to the sea, "Peace! Be still!" The wind ceased, and there was a great calm.
> —Mark 4:39 WEB

Lord Jesus, You stood in the midst of the storm, and with just a word, You arose and rebuked the wind, saying, "Peace, be still." And the wind ceased, and there was a great calm. So now, I come to You—not in my own strength, but trusting in Your voice that still holds all authority.

Speak over the storms in my life, Lord. Where fear howls and chaos rages, speak peace. Where the enemy stirs up confusion, anxiety, or despair, rise and rebuke it with the power of Your word. I believe, Lord, that You are not distant in my trouble. You are in the boat with me. And when You speak, all creation listens.

Silence every voice that is not Yours. Still every wave that crashes against my soul. Command the wind of adversity to bow before You. You are the Prince of Peace, and when You say "be still," nothing can remain in turmoil.

I surrender my restlessness, my fear, my trembling spirit into Your hands. Let Your calm flood my heart. Let Your presence be my anchor. The storm may rage, but You are greater. I trust You, Lord, even in the shaking—because You are the One who speaks peace.

In Jesus' name, Amen.

Day 5: He Rebuked the Sea

> He rebuked the Red Sea also, and it was dried up; so he led them through the depths, as through a desert.
> —Psalms 106:9 WEB

Lord, You rebuked the Red Sea also, and it was dried up—so You led Your people through the depths, as through the wilderness. And today, I remember that same power still goes before me.

You are the God who makes a way when there is no way. When the enemy presses in behind me and impossibilities stretch out before me, You lift Your hand and command the sea to part. You silence the roar of the deep and turn what should have drowned me into a dry path beneath my feet.

I praise You, Lord, for being my Deliverer. You have rebuked the forces that threatened to overwhelm me. You have pushed back the waters of fear, despair, and bondage. What seemed impossible has become the very place of my victory, because You walked me through it.

So I trust You again today. Rebuke the sea before me, Lord. Make a way through every barrier the enemy has raised. Lead me through the depths, and I will follow You into freedom.

Thank You that no tide can overtake me when You are with me. No power of darkness can stop the path You've opened. I walk forward in faith, praising You for the victory already won.

In Jesus' name, Amen.

Day 6: Scatter the Beasts

> Rebuke the wild animal of the reeds, the multitude of the bulls, with the calves of the peoples. Being humbled, may it bring bars of silver. Scatter the nations that delight in war.
> —Psalms 68:30 WEB

Lord, rebuke the company of spearmen, the multitude of the bulls, with the calves of the people, till they submit themselves with silver. Scatter the people that delight in war. You are the God of power and justice, and I call upon You now to rise and defend.

Where the enemy has gathered in pride—where spiritual forces of darkness rage and stir up strife—You, O Lord, are mighty to scatter them. I do not trust in my own strength or wisdom. I look to You, the One who reigns above all, whose voice shakes the heavens and whose word brings down every proud and violent force.

Rebuke every demonic power that seeks to intimidate, to ensnare, or to steal what You've promised me. Bring low the opposition that glories in conflict. Cause them to yield, not by the sword of man, but by the weight of Your presence and the authority of Your throne.

Let every rebellious plan crumble. Let peace be established where war was stirred. You are my Deliverer, and I trust in Your holy name to bring down every proud enemy that exalts itself against Your will for my life.

Thank You, Lord, that I am not alone in this battle. You fight for me. You speak, and Your enemies scatter.

In Jesus' name, Amen.

Day 7: Flee Like Chaff

> The nations will rush like the rushing of many waters: but he will rebuke them, and they will flee far off, and will be chased like the chaff of the mountains before the wind, and like the whirling dust before the storm.
> —Isaiah 17:13 WEB

Lord, the nations may rush like the rushing of many waters, and the enemy may rise like a flood, but when You rebuke them, they flee far off. They are chased like the chaff of the mountains before the wind, and like a rolling thing before the whirlwind.

I stand in awe of Your power, O God. No matter how loud the noise, how fierce the opposition, or how overwhelming the tide—I know that one word from You causes every adversary to scatter. The noise of the nations is nothing before Your voice. You are the One who stills the storm, who shatters the plans of the proud, who drives out every force that rises against Your people.

So I wait in trust, not in fear. Though the enemy stirs and the pressure mounts, I know You will arise and speak. And when You do, confusion will fall upon every dark force. They will flee, tossed and scattered like dust before Your breath.

Rebuke the enemy in my life, Lord. Let Your wind drive out every spirit of fear, oppression, and confusion. Let nothing stand before Your might. Be my defense and my victory. I rest in Your strength, knowing You are near and ready to deliver.

In Jesus' name, Amen.

Day 8: He Rebuked the Unclean Spirit

> While he was still coming, the demon threw him down and convulsed him violently. But Jesus rebuked the unclean spirit, and healed the boy, and gave him back to his father.
> —Luke 9:42 WEB

Lord Jesus, just as the child was coming to You and the devil threw him down and tore him, You rebuked the unclean spirit, healed the child, and delivered him back to his father. I praise You, Lord, because You are still the same today—mighty to rebuke, heal, and restore.

Even when the enemy tries to attack as I draw near to You, even when he tries to tear at me with fear, sickness, confusion, or torment, You do not turn away. You step in with authority. You rebuke every foul spirit. You silence every demonic voice. And You bring healing where there was hurt, peace where there was chaos, and freedom where there was bondage.

Lord, I trust in Your power over every dark force. Rebuke the enemy in my life. Heal the places that have been torn. Restore what has been broken. Just as You delivered that child back whole and free, I believe You will do the same for me.

You are the Deliverer, full of compassion and power. Nothing is too hard for You. I surrender to Your touch, I welcome Your voice, and I receive Your healing today.

In Jesus' name, Amen.

Day 9: THE GREAT VENGEANCE

> I will execute great vengeance on them with wrathful rebukes. Then they will know that I am Yahweh, when I lay my vengeance on them.'"
> —Ezekiel 25:17 WEB

Righteous Father, You have declared that You will execute great vengeance upon them with furious rebukes, and they shall know that You are the Lord when You lay Your vengeance upon them. So I come before You now, not seeking revenge with my own hands, but trusting in Your holy justice to rise on my behalf.

You see the schemes of the enemy. You hear the threats and lies spoken in the dark. You know the oppression and the pain, and You do not forget. You are not silent. You are not still. At the appointed time, You rise with furious rebukes, and every evil force must bow.

Lord, rebuke the enemy who seeks to destroy, who rejoices in injustice and cruelty. Let Your vengeance fall not from hate, but from Your holiness, from Your covenant love for Your people. Defend Your name. Protect Your servant. Prove to every watching spirit that You alone are God.

I stand under Your covering, not to repay evil with evil, but to wait on You. And I will see Your hand move. I will witness the downfall of every force that has defied You. You will show Yourself strong, and all will know that You are the Lord.

In Jesus' name, Amen.

Day 10: WITH FIRE AND SWORD

> For, behold, Yahweh will come with fire, and his chariots will be like the whirlwind; to render his anger with fierceness, and his rebuke with flames of fire.
> —Isaiah 66:15 WEB

Lord God Almighty, I tremble before Your greatness, for behold, You will come with fire, and with Your chariots like a whirlwind, to render Your anger with fury and Your rebuke with flames of fire. You are not a passive God. You are the consuming fire, the righteous Judge, and the holy Defender of Your people.

I do not take lightly the power of Your coming. When You rise, nothing can stand against You. Your rebuke burns away wickedness. Your fury brings justice where evil has long ruled. You do not forget the cries of the oppressed or overlook the mockery of the proud.

So I call on You now—rebuke the enemy with flames of fire. Burn away every dark scheme formed against me. Let the whirlwind of Your Spirit sweep through every stronghold and break every chain. Where the enemy has encamped, let Your fire fall. Where lies have taken root, let truth consume.

I take refuge in Your holy presence. I surrender all fear, for You fight for me. I stand in awe of Your might and rest in the shadow of Your glory. Come, Lord, and let Your fire do its perfect work.

In Jesus' name, Amen.

Day 11: One Shall Chase a Thousand

> One thousand will flee at the threat of one. At the threat of five, you will flee until you are left like a beacon on the top of a mountain, and like a banner on a hill.
> —Isaiah 30:17 WEB

Lord, You have said that one thousand shall flee at the rebuke of one, and at the rebuke of five shall they flee, till we are left as a beacon upon the top of a mountain, and as an ensign on a hill. And so I stand today, not in fear, but in the power of Your promise.

When You rebuke the enemy, Lord, multitudes scatter. What once surrounded me flees in every direction at the sound of Your voice. I don't need to be many. I only need to be Yours. Because even one, standing in Your authority, causes a thousand to run. Even five, anointed by Your Spirit, shake the enemy's camp.

So let every power of darkness that has gathered against me be scattered by Your rebuke. Let every assignment of fear, confusion, or oppression flee. Let me stand, not hidden in defeat, but lifted up as a testimony—like a beacon on a mountain, like a banner of Your faithfulness on a hill.

You are my strength, my covering, and my victory. I trust in Your word, Lord. Let Your rebuke go forth and let Your name be exalted in my life.

In Jesus' name, Amen.

PART 2: Releasing Terror Upon the Enemy

Our God is not only a Shepherd—He is a warrior. When He rises, His enemies scatter. When He speaks, the earth trembles. The enemy may boast and intimidate, but when the presence of the Lord draws near, it is the enemy who trembles in fear.

In this section, we pray in agreement with the holy dread that falls upon those who oppose God's people. We call upon the Lord to send confusion into the camp of the wicked, to release terror that causes the adversary to flee without a fight. This is not a cry for vengeance—it is a cry for divine justice, for the manifestation of God's power that makes His enemies melt like wax before Him.

As you pray these Scriptures, remember: you are not defenseless. You are not outnumbered. The fear of the Lord is your weapon, and the Lord of Hosts is on your side.

Day 12: Terror Fell on Them

> Let's arise, and go up to Bethel. I will make there an altar to God, who answered me in the day of my distress, and was with me on the way which I went." They traveled, and a terror of God was on the cities that were around them, and they didn't pursue the sons of Jacob.
> —Genesis 35: 3, 5 WEB

O God of my house and my journey, I come to You with a heart full of remembrance and trust. You are the One who answered me in the day of my distress and was with me in every place I have gone. When I was weary, You were near. When I was afraid, You did not abandon me. You saw my tears and heard my cries, and You came—faithful and true.

So now, I return to You with gratitude and with confidence. Just as You were with Jacob, You are with me. And as I walk forward, I do not walk alone. You go before me, and at the sound of Your presence, terror falls upon every enemy. They do not rise against me, for Your fear covers the path ahead. You scatter those who would do harm; You disarm those who plot in secret.

Lord, release holy terror upon every force that dares to rise against Your purpose in my life. Not by my strength, but by Your presence— let the enemy be shaken. Let confusion grip their camp. Let dread fall where arrogance once ruled. Let every unclean spirit that follows me or watches me turn and flee at the shadow of Your glory.

I surrender all striving, because You are my Defender. I need not fight as the world fights, for You are the God who terrifies the enemy with just the echo of Your steps. Keep me hidden in You, and surround me with the fire of Your holiness. Let Your fear fall and Your name be lifted high.

In Jesus' name, Amen.

Day 13: Hearts Melted in Fear

> She said to the men, "I know that Yahweh has given you the land, and that the fear of you has fallen upon us, and that all the inhabitants of the land melt away before you. For we have heard how Yahweh dried up the water of the Red Sea before you, when you came out of Egypt; and what you did to the two kings of the Amorites, who were beyond the Jordan, to Sihon and to Og, whom you utterly destroyed. As soon as we had heard it, our hearts melted, and there wasn't any more spirit in any man, because of you: for Yahweh your God, he is God in heaven above, and on earth beneath.
> —Joshua 2:9-11 WEB

Lord God of Heaven and Earth, I lift my heart in awe of who You are. Just as Rahab spoke of You with trembling reverence, I declare today: I know that You have given victory to Your people. The hearts of our enemies melt because of You. Terror has gone out before Your name, for You are the God who dries up seas, who breaks down walls, who delivers with power and purpose.

The enemy has heard of what You've done—how You delivered from bondage, how You conquered kings, how You moved in might—and their courage has failed. So now, Lord, as I engage in battle, I do not fear the strength of those who rise against me, because I know who goes before me.

Release fear into the enemy's camp. Let the memory of what You've done and the power of Your name shake their foundations. Let them tremble, not at me, but at You—the living God who fights for His own.

I surrender to Your will, Lord. I take my place in the victory You have already declared. You are the God in heaven above and in earth beneath, and I rest in the safety of Your presence as You release terror upon every adversary that rises against Your name and Your purpose in my life.

In Jesus' name, Amen.

Day 14: Dread and Awe

> Then the chiefs of Edom were dismayed. Trembling takes hold of the mighty men of Moab. All the inhabitants of Canaan have melted away. Terror and dread falls on them. By the greatness of your arm they are as still as a stone— until your people pass over, Yahweh, until the people you have purchased pass over.
> —Exodus 15:15-16 WEB

Lord, my Strength and my Song, You have become my salvation. Just as the hearts of the nations melted in fear when they heard of Your mighty works, I declare now—there is no one like You. You are the God who brings down proud rulers and causes whole kingdoms to tremble at the sound of Your glory.

Let the leaders of darkness be dismayed. Let every force that exalts itself against You be seized with trembling. As You did in days of old—when fear and dread fell upon the enemies of Israel—do it again, Lord. Let Your presence go before me like fire. Let the enemy be still as stone, unable to move, unable to strike, overwhelmed by the weight of Your power.

Until Your people pass over, O Lord—until I pass over into the place of promise and peace—let Your terror surround the way. Not for destruction, but for deliverance. Not to harm me, but to hold back those who seek my harm. You have covered me with Your hand, and I walk forward in reverent trust.

You are the One who redeems and protects. The One who makes nations tremble and hearts bow. I praise You for Your might, and I rest in Your defense.

In Jesus' name, Amen.

Day 15: Thundered Against the Enemy

> As Samuel was offering up the burnt offering, the Philistines came near to battle against Israel; but Yahweh thundered with a great thunder on that day on the Philistines, and confused them; and they were struck down before Israel.
> —1 Samuel 7:10 WEB

Lord God of Israel, my Deliverer and Defender, I lift my voice to You as Your people once did. While they cried out in offering and trust, You thundered from heaven with a mighty voice and threw the enemy into confusion. You struck fear into their hearts and scattered their plans, all because You were present.

So now, Lord, as I stand in the heat of battle, I bring You my heart, my worship, my surrender. I do not put my trust in weapons or strength, but in You alone. Thunder from heaven on my behalf. Let the sound of Your power shake every force that rises against me. Let confusion fill the enemy's camp. Let their unity be broken and their strength dissolve in fear.

I believe You still speak, and when You do, nothing remains the same. Speak into my situation, Lord. Release Your voice against the darkness. Let Your heavenly roar go before me, disrupting every demonic plan and breaking every chain of oppression.

You are not silent. You are not distant. You are the God who fights for His people—and I am Yours. Cover me in the shadow of Your presence and let every enemy fall before You.

In Jesus' name, Amen.

Day 16: Terrors Overtake Them

> "This is the portion of a wicked man with God, the heritage of oppressors, which they receive from the Almighty. Terrors overtake him like waters. A storm steals him away in the night.
> —Job 27: 13, 20 WEB

Almighty God, righteous and just in all Your ways, I take refuge in the truth of who You are. You see the end of the wicked, and You do not turn a blind eye to evil. This is the portion of the wicked man with God—the inheritance of oppressors—terror shall overtake them like waters, and in the night, a storm shall carry them away.

So I stand in Your justice, O Lord. I do not envy the strength of the wicked, nor do I fear their threats. For though they may rise with pride, You bring them low in an instant. Let the terror they intended for me return upon their own heads. Let the whirlwind of Your judgment awaken them in the night. You are holy, and Your righteousness prevails.

Where evil has flourished, let it now wither. Where the enemy has plotted in secret, let Your storm expose and scatter every plan. Cover me, Lord, while You move in justice. Keep me hidden in Your peace while You deal with the adversary in truth and power.

I trust not in vengeance, but in You. You are my shield, my judge, and my strong deliverer. Let every rising threat be silenced, and let Your righteousness be seen.

In Jesus' name, Amen.

Day 17: DRIVEN TO DARKNESS

> "Yes, the light of the wicked shall be put out, The spark of his fire shall not shine. Terrors shall make him afraid on every side, and shall chase him at his heels.
> —Job 18: 5, 11 WEB

O Lord, Light of my life and Shield of my soul, I thank You that the light of the wicked shall be put out, and the spark of their fire shall not shine. No weapon formed against me shall prosper, because You are the One who extinguishes every false light and silences every lying voice.

The enemy may boast, may burn for a moment with pride and intimidation—but You, O God, will snuff out their flame. You will darken their path and scatter their plans. Let fear—the very terror they hoped to bring upon me—seize them on every side. Let dread, not from man, but from Your holiness, surround them like a flood.

You are my refuge, Lord. I will not fear, though darkness presses near. Because You are light, and in You is no shadow of turning. The path of the righteous shines brighter and brighter, but the way of the wicked is darkened by Your hand.

Cover me with Your presence. Guard my heart from fear. Let the enemy's strength dissolve in Your justice, and let my soul rest in the confidence of Your protection.

In Jesus' name, Amen.

Day 18: THE ARROWS OF THE ALMIGHTY

> For the arrows of the Almighty are within me. My spirit drinks up their poison. The terrors of God set themselves in array against me.
> —Job 6:4 WEB

Lord, my God, You know the depths of my pain, the weight that words cannot express. Like Job, I feel the piercing of arrows—not from men, but from the heaviness of affliction that presses on my spirit. Your arrows are within me, and the poison of fear, grief, and sorrow seems to drink up my strength. The terrors of God set themselves in array against me, and I feel surrounded.

But even in this, I come to You—not to hide, but to surrender. You are still my refuge, even when I don't understand. You are still good, even when the pain is sharp. I trust You, Lord, not because I feel strong, but because I know You are near to the brokenhearted and You save those crushed in spirit.

Though I feel wounded, I will not turn from You. Though the weight is great, I lay it down before Your throne. Teach me to find peace in Your presence, even in the storm. Let the bitterness drain away, and let Your healing begin its work in the deepest places of my soul.

You are the God who sees, the God who knows, and the God who heals. So I rest in You now. Hold me, carry me, and remind me that nothing I face is beyond Your reach.

In Jesus' name, Amen.

Day 19: Terrors Turn Upon Me

> Terrors have turned on me. They chase my honor as the wind.
> My welfare has passed away as a cloud.
> —Job 30:15 WEB

Lord, I come to You in the midst of the storm within. Terrors are turned upon me; they chase me like a fierce wind, and my soul feels poured out like water. I confess, God—there are moments when strength fails and hope seems distant. The enemy surrounds me with whispers of fear, shadows of shame, and waves of discouragement. But even now, I lift my eyes to You.

You are the One who steadies me when everything else gives way. Though the wind howls and the night is long, You are my anchor. I will not be swept away, for You hold me fast. When my dignity is stripped and my defense feels gone, You clothe me with mercy and cover me with peace.

Rebuke the terrors, Lord. Drive them back with the breath of Your mouth. Let every force that has risen against my soul be scattered in confusion. I may feel emptied, but I know You are the God who fills. I may feel pursued, but You are the God who surrounds me with songs of deliverance.

Restore to me what the enemy has tried to take. Breathe new life into the dry places of my soul. Lift my head once more, and let Your presence be my comfort and my confidence.

In Jesus' name, Amen.

Day 20: The Sound of Dread

> A sound of terrors is in his ears. In prosperity the destroyer shall come on him.
> —Job 15:21 WEB

Lord God, You know the heart of every person, and nothing is hidden from Your sight. You have said there is a dreadful sound in the ears of the wicked, and that in prosperity, the destroyer shall come upon them. So I take comfort not in the fall of others, but in the assurance that You are a God of justice who sees every secret motive, every hidden threat, and every proud voice raised against Your people.

I trust You to be my shield and my strong tower. While the wicked live in fear of judgment, I rest in Your mercy. While the destroyer comes unexpectedly to those who defy You, I abide in the shadow of the Almighty. You silence the dreadful sounds in the night, and You guard my heart from the terror that haunts others.

Lord, release that fear and dread upon the enemy—those spiritual forces that war against my soul. Let the sound of their own destruction echo in their ears. Let them tremble in the darkness they once used to intimidate. And let them know that You, the Holy One, reign in power and truth.

Keep me in the peace that only You give. Let no fear grip my heart, for I am hidden in You. Let Your justice roll down like waters, and Your righteousness like a mighty stream.

In Jesus' name, Amen.

Day 21: The Sound of Panic

> For the Lord had made the army of the Syrians to hear the sound of chariots, and the sound of horses, even the noise of a great army; and they said to one another, "Behold, the king of Israel has hired against us the kings of the Hittites and the kings of the Egyptians to attack us." Therefore they arose and fled in the twilight, and left their tents, and their horses, and their donkeys, even the camp as it was, and fled for their life.
> —2 Kings 7:6-7 WEB

Lord God of Hosts, You are the God who confounds the enemy without a sword being lifted. Just as You caused the army of the Syrians to hear the noise of chariots and horses—the sound of a great host—and they fled in terror, leaving behind everything they had, I call upon You now to release confusion into the camp of every force that rises against me.

You are the God who speaks, and the enemy runs. You are the One who causes fear to fall where pride once stood. Let every demonic power, every oppressing spirit, every scheme of darkness hear the sound of Your heavenly army and scatter in dread. Let them abandon their plans, their weapons, and their positions, because You, O Lord, have drawn near.

What I could not fight in my own strength, You have already overcome by the power of Your word. Just as You brought supernatural fear upon the enemy, do it again, Lord. Let confusion, panic, and divine terror overthrow every assignment formed against my life, my home, and my purpose.

I trust You, my Deliverer. The battle belongs to You. While I stand in stillness, You thunder in the unseen realm. And I will walk forward into what the enemy left behind—blessings untouched, territory reclaimed, and peace restored—because You have fought for me. In Jesus' name, Amen.

Day 22: Fear on Every Side

> Now Pashhur, the son of Immer the priest, who was chief officer in Yahweh's house, heard Jeremiah prophesying these things. Then Pashhur struck Jeremiah the prophet, and put him in the stocks that were in the upper gate of Benjamin, which was in Yahweh's house. On the next day, Pashhur released Jeremiah out of the stocks. Then Jeremiah said to him, "Yahweh has not called your name Pashhur, but Magormissabib. For Yahweh says, 'Behold, I will make you a terror to yourself and to all your friends. They will fall by the sword of their enemies, and your eyes will see it. I will give all Judah into the hand of the king of Babylon, and he will carry them captive to Babylon, and will kill them with the sword.
> —Jeremiah 20:1-4 WEB

O Lord of Hosts, who knows all hearts and sees every hidden motive, I come before You with trust in Your justice and confidence in Your Word. Just as You saw the pride and mockery of Pashur, who struck Jeremiah and sought to silence the voice of truth, You also see every force that rises up to oppose Your purpose in my life.

You declared that Pashur would no longer be called by his name, but "Magor-missabib"—terror on every side. So now, Lord, I call upon You: release that same terror upon the enemy. Let every spirit of intimidation, every tongue of accusation, every hand lifted in rebellion against Your truth be overtaken by dread. Let those who seek to oppress, to shame, or to wound Your servants find themselves surrounded by the fear they once tried to inflict.

You are the Righteous Judge, and You will cause every corrupt power to fall. What was done in darkness will be exposed in light. What was meant to harm will be turned for deliverance. And those who once sat in pride will be brought low by the weight of Your truth.

I stand in surrender, not seeking revenge, but trusting in Your justice. Fight for me, Lord. Defend my cause. And may Your holy fear be released wherever Your name is defied and Your Word is resisted.

In Jesus' name, Amen.

Day 23: Sudden Destruction

> Surely you set them in slippery places. You throw them down to destruction. How they are suddenly destroyed! They are completely swept away with terrors.
>
> —Psalms 73:18-19 WEB

Lord, my Refuge and my Righteous King, I come before You in reverent awe. Truly, You have set the wicked in slippery places; You cast them down into destruction. How they are brought into desolation—as in a moment! They are utterly consumed with terrors.

I take no delight in their downfall, but I find peace in knowing that You are just. You see every act of pride, every word of mockery, every scheme plotted in secret—and You are not silent. Though they seemed secure in their rebellion, You caused their footing to vanish beneath them. At Your appointed time, You arise, and all that is false crumbles.

So, Lord, I trust You. When the enemy appears strong, remind me of how quickly You can bring their power to nothing. When fear tries to grip my heart, remind me that terror belongs to those who oppose You, not to those who take refuge in You.

Keep me in humility. Keep me in worship. While others are consumed with fear, let me be consumed with Your presence. You are my stronghold in the day of trouble, and in You I am safe.

In Jesus' name, Amen.

Day 24: THE BRONZE DRAWN SWORD

> When he is about to fill his belly, God will cast the fierceness of his wrath on him. It will rain on him while he is eating. He shall flee from the iron weapon. The bronze arrow shall strike him through. He draws it out, and it comes out of his body. Yes, the glittering point comes out of his liver. Terrors are on him.
> —Job 20:23-25 WEB

Lord God, Righteous Judge and Avenger of the oppressed, I trust in the justice of Your throne. You see the wicked when they fill their belly, when they boast in abundance and think themselves secure. But You, O Lord, will cast the fury of Your wrath upon them, and while they feast in pride, You rain it upon them without warning.

Your arrows are sharp and sure. When they draw near to strike, it is they who are pierced. The sword comes out of their own armor, and the glittering point comes out from their gall. Terrors take hold of them, and their confidence collapses like dust in the wind.

I will not fear the rise of the wicked, nor envy their moment of prosperity. For You, O Lord, have appointed a day when justice will be revealed. Every lie will be exposed, every cruelty answered, every weapon turned back upon the hands that formed it.

Cover me in the day of Your justice. Let not my heart be shaken by the schemes of darkness, but let it be anchored in the truth of Your Word. You fight for the righteous. You see, You act, and You never forget.

I rest in Your power, Lord, and I walk in peace—even when surrounded—because You are the One who defends and delivers.

In Jesus' name, Amen.

Day 25: Terror Within and Without

> Outside the sword will bereave, and in the rooms, terror; on both young man and virgin, the nursing infant with the gray-haired man.
> —Deuteronomy 32:25 WEB

Most High God, Defender of the covenant and Avenger of the innocent, I come before You in holy fear and trembling trust. You are the One who judges righteously and repays those who rise up in rebellion against You. Your Word declares that the sword shall devour without, and terror within, destroying both the young man and the maiden, the nursing child and the man of gray hairs.

You are not mocked. What is sown in wickedness shall be reaped in judgment. Those who defy You, who oppress, who harm the innocent and walk in arrogance—You will bring them low. Terror shall arise from within their walls, and the sword of divine justice shall not miss its mark.

So I call upon You now, Lord—release holy dread upon every force of darkness that wars against Your people. Let terror rise in the hearts of the unrepentant, not to destroy for destruction's sake, but that they may know You are God. Let every arrogant heart tremble. Let every unclean spirit be driven out by the sword of Your Word.

Cover me under the shadow of Your wings. Keep me in the shelter of Your mercy, while You move in justice. I will not fear the weapons of the enemy, for You are the One who commands every battle and reigns over every storm.

In Jesus' name, Amen.

Day 26: He Shall Cut Down the Branches

> Behold, the Lord, Yahweh of Armies, will lop the boughs with terror. The tall will be cut down, and the lofty will be brought low.
> —Isaiah 10:33 WEB

Lord God of Hosts, Mighty One who rules with power and righteousness, I bow before You in awe. You are the One who brings low the haughty and strikes down the proud with a swift hand. As You have said, You shall cut down the branches with terror; the high ones of stature shall be cut down, and the proud shall be humbled.

So now, Lord, I trust in Your justice. Where the enemy has exalted himself, raise Your hand. Where pride has reached toward heaven, cut it down with holy fear. Let every spiritual force that towers in arrogance against You be brought to nothing. Let every scheme built on pride be dismantled by the power of Your presence.

You are not a passive God. You arise with fire in Your voice and strength in Your arm. You see the oppression. You hear the cries of the righteous. And You move—not slowly, but with might—to humble what man has exalted.

Cut down the enemy, Lord—not with cruelty, but with justice. Humble every power that resists You, and establish Your name as holy in all the earth. I take refuge in You, the One who defends the lowly and brings justice to the afflicted.

In Jesus' name, Amen.

Day 27: THE FEAR OF JUDAH

> In that day the Egyptians will be like women. They will tremble and fear because of the shaking of Yahweh of Armies's hand, which he shakes over them. The land of Judah will become a terror to Egypt. Everyone to whom mention is made of it will be afraid, because of the plans of Yahweh of Armies, which he determines against it.
> —Isaiah 19:16-17 WEB

Lord God of Hosts, Holy and Awesome is Your name. You have declared that in that day, Egypt shall be like unto women—fearful and trembling under the hand You lift against them. The very land shall shake at Your presence, and terror shall seize those who once stood in defiance. The name of Judah, the name of Your people, shall be a terror unto them, because of the purpose You have set against them.

So now, O Lord, rise and stretch out Your hand. Let every enemy that has mocked Your name and oppressed Your people be filled with dread. Let trembling fall upon every power of darkness that has stood against Your will. Where once there was pride, let there now be fear. Where there was arrogance, let there be brokenness before You.

Cause the enemy to melt with fear at the sound of Your name. Let the land of opposition shake at Your purpose. Not by human might, but by Your Spirit—release Your holy terror upon every spiritual adversary that resists the advance of Your kingdom in my life.

I stand firm, not in my own strength, but in the assurance that You are with me. The enemy will fear, not me, but You, O Lord, who dwell in the midst of Your people with glory and power.

In Jesus' name, Amen.

Day 28: Great Fear Where None Was

> Have the workers of iniquity no knowledge, who eat up my people as they eat bread, and don't call on God? There they were in great fear, where no fear was, for God has scattered the bones of him who encamps against you. You have put them to shame, because God has rejected them.
> —Psalms 53:4-5 WEB

O Lord, my Righteous King, I lift my heart to You in holy trust. Your Word declares that the workers of iniquity—those who devour Your people as if they were bread, who call not upon Your name—shall be overcome with great fear, where no fear was before. For You, O God, are in the generation of the righteous.

I take refuge in this truth: that though the enemy may seem bold and unshaken, a day comes when You will cause terror to fall upon them. Where they felt secure in their schemes, You will strike fear into their hearts. Where they mocked and devoured, You will rise in defense of Your people.

Lord, release holy dread upon every spirit that lifts itself against Your name. Let those who plot against the righteous tremble, not at us, but at You. Let fear invade their false peace, and confusion shatter their unity. You are our Defender, and You dwell with those who walk in truth.

Though the enemy may not call upon Your name, I do. I cry out to You, Lord of Hosts—scatter the wicked, deliver Your people, and let Your presence be known in the camp of the enemy. Let fear grip every force that seeks to devour what You have redeemed.

I stand, not in fear, but in faith—because You are with me.

In Jesus' name, Amen.

Day 29: Not Afraid by Night

> You shall not be afraid of the terror by night, nor of the arrow that flies by day;
> —Psalms 91:5 WEB

Most High God, my Refuge and my Fortress, I rest under the shadow of Your wings. Because I dwell in Your secret place, I will not be afraid of the terror by night. You, O Lord, are my covering when darkness falls. You are my shield when silence surrounds, and I will not fear what hides in the shadows.

The night may be full of unseen dangers, but You are with me. When others lie awake in anxiety, I sleep in peace. Not because I am strong, but because You are. You guard my soul. You station angels around me. You speak peace into the very hour fear tries to speak loudest.

Let the terrors of the night be scattered by the light of Your presence. Let every whisper of fear be silenced by the truth of Your Word. I am not alone. I am not uncovered. I am hidden in You—safe, kept, and unshaken.

I will not fear, because You have commanded it. And what You command, You empower. Fill me with boldness. Wrap me in Your love. And let every shadow flee at the mention of Your name.

In Jesus' name, Amen.

Day 30: Far from Oppression

> In righteousness you will be established. You will be far from oppression, for you will not be afraid; and far from terror, for it shall not come near you.
> —Isaiah 54:14 WEB

Righteous Father, my Rock and my Redeemer, I thank You that You have established me in righteousness. Not by my own works, but by the gift of Your mercy and the covering of Your grace. Because of You, I am far from oppression—fear does not rule over me, and terror cannot come near.

You have spoken it, Lord, and I believe it: I am secure in You. The voice of fear may try to whisper, the enemy may attempt to intimidate, but I stand firm, rooted in the righteousness You have placed upon me. No weapon of fear, no scheme of darkness, has authority here.

Drive out every trace of dread from my heart. Let the peace of Your presence rule within me. I am far from terror because You are near. I walk in the confidence of Your promises and sleep in the safety of Your love.

Surround me, Lord, with songs of deliverance. Let every lie be silenced by truth. Let every shadow be pierced by Your light. I am not afraid, because You are the One who upholds me with justice and crowns me with peace.

In Jesus' name, Amen.

Day 31: SANCTIFY THE LORD

> "Don't say, 'A conspiracy!' concerning all about which this people say, 'A conspiracy!' neither fear their threats, nor be terrorized. Yahweh of Armies is who you must respect as holy. He is the one you must fear. He is the one you must dread.
> —Isaiah 8:12-13 WEB

Lord of Hosts, Holy and Sovereign, I set my heart to fear no conspiracy, no threat, no alliance formed against me. The world may call it fear, may tremble at voices and plots in the dark—but I will not be shaken. You have told me not to say, "A confederacy," when the people do, nor to fear what they fear.

Instead, I sanctify You in my heart. You, O Lord, are the One I fear. You are the One I reverence. You are the One I trust. Let Your holy fear rise within me, greater than any fear the enemy tries to stir. Let Your presence be my dread—not in terror, but in awe—knowing that You alone are in control.

I refuse to bow to fear or intimidation. I do not follow the panic of the world. I follow You. You are my sanctuary, my defense, my unshakable foundation. While others may be moved, I remain secure, because I stand in the fear of the Lord.

Set me apart in faith. Guard my heart from compromise. Let the fear of the Lord be my courage and my covering.

In Jesus' name, Amen.

PART 3: Praying for the Fall of the Enemy

God's justice does not sleep. Though the enemy may seem strong, established, or untouchable, every high thing that exalts itself against the knowledge of God will fall. Scripture is clear: the wicked stumble, the proud are brought low, and those who oppose the plans of the Lord are cast down in due time.

In this section, we align our prayers with the righteous judgments of God. We do not pray for harm—we pray for divine disruption. We call upon the Lord to expose, dismantle, and bring to nothing every scheme of darkness. We ask Him to make His justice visible and to bring the downfall of every work that hinders His purpose in our lives and in the world.

The fall of the enemy is not our triumph—it is God's glory revealed. These prayers are not fueled by revenge, but by reverence. As we intercede, we stand in the confidence that every enemy of righteousness will bow before the throne of the Holy One.

Day 32: TURNED BACK AND DESTROYED

> When my enemies turn back, they stumble and perish in your presence. For you have maintained my just cause. You sit on the throne judging righteously.
>
> —Psalms 9:3-4 WEB

Lord, my Righteous Judge and my Strong Defender, I thank You for the assurance of Your justice. When my enemies turn back, they stumble and perish at Your presence. You, O Lord, are not distant from my struggle. You have taken up my cause. You have sat upon Your throne, judging right.

I surrender my fears to You. I don't need to chase vengeance or prove myself, because You are the One who pleads my case. You see every injustice, every lie spoken, every trap set. And when You rise, the enemy cannot stand. At the light of Your face, their strength fails and their schemes unravel.

Thank You for going before me, for defending me without fail. I rest in the truth that my victory is found not in my hands, but in Yours. You vindicate me. You silence the accuser. You declare what is true, and You cause the wicked to fall under the weight of their own pride.

So I lift my eyes to You, trusting in Your righteous rule. Let every enemy turn back in confusion. Let them fall—not by my might—but by the power of Your presence. I will wait on You, worship You, and walk in peace, knowing that You have already secured the victory.

In Jesus' name, Amen.

Day 33: We Rise and Stand Upright

> Some trust in chariots, and some in horses, but we trust the name of Yahweh our God. They are bowed down and fallen, but we rise up, and stand upright.
> —Psalms 20:7-8 WEB

Lord, my Trust and my Banner, I lift my heart to You, for some trust in chariots and some in horses—but I remember the name of the Lord my God. Others may rely on strength, numbers, or strategy, but I anchor my hope in You alone. Your name is my shelter, my confidence, and my victory.

When the enemy rises with pride, when they boast in their own power, they are brought down and fallen. But I stand and rise because I lean on You. You uphold me when I'm weak. You lift me when I stumble. You are the One who causes me to endure when others fall.

I surrender every temptation to fight in my own strength. I lay down my weapons of the flesh and take up the shield of faith. You are my Deliverer, and in You I will not be moved.

Let every force that opposes Your purpose in my life collapse under the weight of its own arrogance. And let me stand, not in pride, but in humble dependence on Your power.

In Jesus' name, Amen.

Day 34: SURE DOWNFALL

> Haman recounted to Zeresh his wife and all his friends everything that had happened to him. Then his wise men and Zeresh his wife said to him, "If Mordecai, before whom you have begun to fall, is of Jewish descent, you will not prevail against him, but you will surely fall before him."
> —Esther 6:13 WEB

Sovereign Lord, You are the God who sees all and turns every hidden plan to serve Your purpose. Just as Haman's wife and friends discerned that he could not prevail against Mordecai because he was of the seed of the Jews, I declare today that those who rise against me cannot stand—for I belong to You.

I am marked by Your covenant, covered by Your mercy, and upheld by Your hand. No plot, no position of power, no prideful scheme can succeed against one You have called and chosen. When the enemy sets himself to destroy, You overturn his plans. You expose his pride, and You bring him low before the eyes of all.

So I rest in the truth that my identity in You makes the enemy's downfall certain. Let every voice that mocks be silenced by Your justice. Let every scheme unravel by Your design. Cause those who oppose me to see that they do not war against flesh and blood—but against the hand of the Living God who defends His own.

You are my shield. You are my vindication. And I stand still, trusting You to bring the downfall of every enemy that rises against Your purpose in my life.

In Jesus' name, Amen.

Day 35: They Went Backward and Fell

> Judas then, having taken a detachment of soldiers and officers from the chief priests and the Pharisees, came there with lanterns, torches, and weapons. Jesus therefore, knowing all the things that were happening to him, went out, and said to them, "Who are you looking for?" They answered him, "Jesus of Nazareth." Jesus said to them, "I am he." Judas also, who betrayed him, was standing with them. When therefore he said to them, "I am he," they went backward, and fell to the ground.
> —John 18:3-6 WEB

Lord Jesus, Mighty Savior and Sovereign King, I stand in awe of Your power and authority. When the band of soldiers and officers came with lanterns, torches, and weapons to seize You, You did not run. You stepped forward and asked, "Whom seek ye?" And when You spoke Your name—"I am He"—they drew back and fell to the ground.

At the sound of Your voice, armed men collapsed. At the revelation of who You are, the strength of the enemy was broken. So now, Lord, I trust in that same power. The enemy may come with threats and numbers, with fear and intimidation—but one word from You is enough to make them fall.

I stand in the shadow of Your strength, not shaken, not afraid. Because You go before me, and when You speak, darkness trembles. Speak over my battle now. Let every force that comes to arrest Your purpose in me be struck down by the authority of Your name. Let Your presence break their formation and scatter their intent.

You are not a victim, Lord—you are the Victor. And I am hidden in You. I walk in Your name, I speak in Your authority, and I rest in the power that causes enemies to fall at the sound of who You are.

In Jesus' name, Amen.

Day 36: SATAN FELL LIKE LIGHTNING

> He said to them, "I saw Satan having fallen like lightning from heaven."
> —Luke 10:18 WEB

Lord Jesus, Victorious One, I praise You, for You said, "I beheld Satan as lightning fall from heaven." You saw the enemy's pride shattered, his throne cast down, his power broken in the presence of true authority—Your authority.

I rejoice in this truth: the enemy is a defeated foe. He may still roam and rage, but he no longer reigns. His fall was swift, and his end is sure. You have triumphed, and in You, I share that victory. No force of darkness can stand against the One who cast Satan down like lightning.

So I stand in the confidence of Your victory, not trembling, but trusting. Not retreating, but advancing in faith. Let every lie the enemy speaks be silenced by this truth—he has fallen, and You are risen. Let every shadow that lingers be driven out by the light of Your glory.

Thank You, Lord, for the authority You've given me in Your name. I will not fear the enemy, because You have already seen him fall.

In Jesus' name, Amen.

Day 37: WHEN THE WICKED CAME

> By David. Yahweh is my light and my salvation. Whom shall I fear? Yahweh is the strength of my life. Of whom shall I be afraid? When evildoers came at me to eat up my flesh, even my adversaries and my foes, they stumbled and fell.
> —Psalms 27:1-2 WEB

Lord, You are my light and my salvation—whom shall I fear? You are the strength of my life—of whom shall I be afraid? I lift my heart to You with confidence, for You have never failed me, and You never will.

When the wicked, even my enemies and my foes, came upon me to eat up my flesh, they stumbled and fell. Not because of my strength, but because of Yours. You go before me. You stand beside me. You cover me from behind. The enemy may come with force, but they cannot stand in the presence of Your glory.

You are my sanctuary when darkness surrounds. You are my courage when fear tries to take hold. I will not be moved, because You are my Light—guiding me, protecting me, lifting me above every threat.

So now, Lord, I choose trust over fear. I choose faith over panic. And I stand, knowing that every enemy that rises against me will stumble and fall—not by my might, but by the power of Your hand.

In Jesus' name, Amen.

Day 38: LET GOD ARISE

For the Chief Musician. A Psalm by David. A song. Let God arise! Let his enemies be scattered! Let them who hate him also flee before him. As smoke is driven away, so drive them away. As wax melts before the fire, so let the wicked perish at the presence of God.
—Psalms 68:1-2 WEB

Almighty God, let You arise, and let every enemy be scattered. Let those who hate You flee before Your presence. As smoke is driven away, so drive them away. As wax melts before the fire, let the wicked perish at the presence of the Lord.

You are not a silent God. You are the God who moves with power, who steps into the battle and makes Your presence known. When You arise, confusion falls on the enemy. When You appear, darkness flees and no evil can stand.

So I call upon You now—rise up, O Lord. Scatter the forces that surround me. Disrupt every demonic plan, overthrow every spirit that resists Your will in my life. Let fear grip the hearts of the adversary. Let their unity crumble, their schemes melt like wax before the heat of Your holiness.

I rest in the truth that You fight for me. I do not stand alone, for the God of heaven goes before me. Let the earth know, let the enemy see—that when You arise, there is no power that can stand against You.

In Jesus' name, Amen.

Day 39: Subdued Under My Feet

> You have enlarged my steps under me, My feet have not slipped. I will pursue my enemies, and overtake them. Neither will I turn again until they are consumed. I will strike them through, so that they will not be able to rise. They shall fall under my feet. For you have armed me with strength to the battle. You have subdued under me those who rose up against me. You have also made my enemies turn their backs to me, that I might cut off those who hate me. Then I beat them small as the dust before the wind. I cast them out as the mire of the streets.
> —Psalms 18: 36-40, 42 WEB

Lord, my Strength and my Deliverer, You have enlarged my steps under me, so that my feet did not slip. When the path was narrow and the battle fierce, You made room for me to stand firm. You armed me with strength for the fight and subdued those that rose up against me. You didn't just protect me—you gave me the victory.

You delivered my enemies into my hands. Those who came against me in pride were brought low beneath Your power. I pursued them in Your name, and they could not rise again. You covered me with the shield of Your salvation, and by Your hand, I overcame.

They cried for help, but none could save them—not even the gods they trusted. And I beat them as small as the dust before the wind. I cast them out like dirt in the streets, for You gave me power over the adversary. Not because I am mighty, but because You are.

So I praise You, Lord. I walk in the authority You have given me. I do not fear the enemy, for You have made me more than a conqueror. Let every power of darkness know that I stand in the victory of the Lord.

In Jesus' name, Amen.

Day 40: No One Shall Stand

> He will deliver their kings into your hand, and you shall make their name perish from under the sky. No one will be able to stand before you, until you have destroyed them.
> —Deuteronomy 7:24 WEB

Lord God, Mighty and Faithful, I praise You for the victory You promise to Your people. You have given over our enemies into our hands, and You cause their names to be wiped out from under heaven. None can stand before You—none can resist the power of Your outstretched arm.

I trust in Your Word, that You will not only drive out those who rise against me, but You will cause them to fall before me. Every force that exalts itself against Your purpose—bring it low. Every voice that resists Your truth—silence it. You are the God who removes every stronghold and gives no place for the enemy to stand.

I will not fear their numbers, their names, or their pride. For You have said they shall be utterly destroyed and remembered no more. I walk in Your promise. I stand in the authority of Your covenant.

Let the name of the enemy be forgotten, and let Your name be exalted forever in my life. Thank You for going before me and for giving me the victory.

In Jesus' name, Amen.

Day 41: Fallen Suddenly

> Whoever walks blamelessly is kept safe; but one with perverse ways will fall suddenly.
> —Proverbs 28:18 WEB

Righteous Father, Keeper of my path, I thank You that You watch over those who walk in integrity. You have promised that whoever walks uprightly shall be saved—and I cling to that promise today. Though the enemy lays snares and temptations all around me, I fix my heart on walking in truth, led by Your Spirit and guarded by Your grace.

You are my safeguard against the traps of the wicked. You steady my steps when the way is narrow. And even when I stumble, You lift me with mercy and surround me with light. I will not fear the fall of the enemy, for You uphold the upright—but the crooked will be cast down in a moment.

Lord, keep me in the way of righteousness. Let my heart be clean, my motives pure, and my spirit yielded fully to You. While the wicked fall suddenly and without warning, let me walk securely in Your salvation.

I surrender again to Your leading, and I trust You to preserve me.

In Jesus' name, Amen.

Day 42: SLIPPERY PLACES

> Surely you set them in slippery places. You throw them down to destruction. How they are suddenly destroyed! They are completely swept away with terrors.
> —Psalms 73:18-19 WEB

Lord, my Sovereign and Righteous King, I come before You in awe of Your wisdom and justice. Truly, You have set the wicked in slippery places; You cast them down into destruction. They rise in pride, boasting in their strength, yet in a moment—they are brought to nothing.

How suddenly they are consumed, O God! Their fall is swift, their ruin complete. What seemed secure was only illusion, for without You, there is no lasting ground. Their arrogance melts in the light of Your holiness, and their plans dissolve like smoke.

But I will not envy their prosperity. I will not fear their threats. You are my portion forever, and I trust in the security of Your presence. While they are consumed with terrors, I am kept in perfect peace. While they fall into ruin, I stand on the Rock that never moves.

Thank You, Lord, for being my sure foundation. Let every enemy that opposes Your purpose be brought low, not by my hand, but by the weight of Your glory. I rest in the victory that belongs to You.

In Jesus' name, Amen.

Day 43: CHASED BY THE ANGEL OF THE LORD

> Let those who seek after my soul be disappointed and brought to dishonor. Let those who plot my ruin be turned back and confounded. Let them be as chaff before the wind, Yahweh's angel driving them on. Let their way be dark and slippery, Yahweh's angel pursuing them.
> —Psalms 35:4-6 WEB

Lord, my Defender and my Righteous Judge, I lift my voice to You in trust and surrender. Let those who seek after my soul be confounded and put to shame. Let those who devise hurt against me be turned back and brought to confusion. Not because of my strength, but because of Your faithfulness and justice.

You see every hidden snare, every lying tongue, every proud heart that rises against Your servant. You do not sit idly by. You arise with holy vengeance—not out of cruelty, but out of covenant love. So let them be as chaff before the wind, driven away by the breath of Your mouth. Let the angel of the Lord chase them, scattering their steps and breaking their schemes.

Make their path dark and slippery, Lord—not so they are destroyed, but so they are stopped. So they can no longer carry out evil against the righteous. You are the One who lifts the lowly and resists the proud. You are the One who vindicates those who wait on You.

I will not fear, for You fight for me. I will not retaliate, for You are my justice. I will wait on You, confident that the enemies of righteousness will not prevail.

In Jesus' name, Amen.

Day 44: In Due Time

> Vengeance is mine, and recompense, at the time when their foot slides; for the day of their calamity is at hand. Their doom rushes at them."
> —Deuteronomy 32:35 WEB

Righteous and Holy God, I bow before You in reverent awe. You have declared, "To Me belongs vengeance and recompence; their foot shall slide in due time." You see every injustice, every act of pride, every hand lifted against the innocent. And You have not forgotten. You are not slow to act—You are patient, and Your justice is sure.

I do not take vengeance into my own hands, Lord. I trust You. I release every wrong, every wound, every enemy into Your care. For their day of judgment will come, and in due time, their fall will be swift. You will repay, not in anger like man, but in perfect righteousness. You will act when their time has come, and nothing can stay Your hand.

So I rest in Your justice, Lord. I choose peace over bitterness, faith over retaliation. You are my Defender. You are my Advocate. And I know the day will come when every wrong is made right by You.

Until then, I remain in the shelter of Your mercy, walking in the light of Your truth.

In Jesus' name, Amen.

Day 45: Slippery Darkness

> Therefore their way will be to them as slippery places in the darkness. They will be driven on, and fall therein; for I will bring evil on them, even the year of their visitation," says Yahweh.
> —Jeremiah 23:12 WEB

Holy and Just God, You see what is hidden, and You expose every path that leads away from truth. You have declared that for those who walk in deception and rebellion, their way shall be unto them as slippery places in the darkness. They shall be driven on and fall therein, for You will bring evil upon them in the time of their visitation.

I trust in Your righteousness, Lord. When the enemy walks in arrogance, cloaked in falsehood and deceit, You are not blind. You will not allow injustice to stand forever. Let their path become what they have chosen—a dark and slippery road where their own feet fail them. Let every plan born of wickedness collapse under its own weight.

While they fall in the darkness of their own making, I will walk in the light of Your truth. You are my sure footing, my steady ground. You guide the upright, and You bring down every high place that exalts itself against You.

I do not gloat in their fall, but I rejoice in Your justice. You are holy, You are faithful, and You will act in Your perfect time. Keep me in humility and guard my steps, that I may walk always in the fear of the Lord.

In Jesus' name, Amen.

Day 46: Stumble in the Dark

> The way of the wicked is like darkness. They don't know what they stumble over.
> —Proverbs 4:19 WEB

Lord, my Light and my Guide, I thank You that You have not left me to walk in darkness. Your Word says the way of the wicked is as darkness—they know not at what they stumble. But I praise You, for You have called me out of that darkness into Your marvelous light.

I lift up my soul to You, asking for discernment and truth. Let the path of the wicked remain dark and exposed. Let them stumble not by accident, but because their ways are false and their hearts resist Your truth. Let every plan formed in darkness collapse before it can bear fruit. You are the One who frustrates the schemes of the ungodly.

I will not envy their steps, for though they may move quickly, they walk blindly. Though they may seem strong, they cannot see what lies ahead. But You, O Lord, make my path straight. You give light to my eyes and wisdom to my heart.

Keep me from that way, Lord. Lead me ever in the path of righteousness, and cause the works of darkness to fall before the brilliance of Your glory.

In Jesus' name, Amen.

PART 4: Treading Upon The Enemy

There comes a time in spiritual warfare when the believer moves from defense to dominion. Through Christ, we have not only been rescued—we have been authorized. We are not called to cower, but to conquer. The enemy is not just to be resisted, but trampled underfoot.

In this section, we stand on the promises of God that declare our victory through Christ. We pray with holy confidence, knowing that God has placed all things under Jesus' feet—and we, as His Body, share in that triumph. These are not passive prayers—they are active declarations of authority, forged in the fire of Scripture and backed by the power of heaven.

To tread upon the enemy is to walk in the finished work of the cross, crushing fear, breaking oppression, and silencing every voice that rises against the truth. It is to declare, with every step, that the kingdom of darkness has no place here.

Take your place. Lift your voice. And tread boldly.

Day 47: Watch Me Rise

> Don't rejoice against me, my enemy. When I fall, I will arise. When I sit in darkness, Yahweh will be a light to me. Then my enemy will see it, and shame will cover her who said to me, where is Yahweh your God? Then my enemy will see me and will cover her shame. Now she will be trodden down like the mire of the streets.
> —Micah 7: 8, 10 WEB

Lord, my Light and my Salvation, though I have fallen, I will rise. Though I sit in darkness, I know that You are a light unto me. My soul clings to this hope—that You do not cast me off forever, and that even in the valley, You are near. When the enemy mocks me, saying, "Where is your God?" I will not answer in fear, for You, O Lord, are still on the throne.

You see my struggle. You know my sorrow. And yet You are the One who lifts me up from the dust and strengthens my feet for the path ahead. You will plead my cause, and You will execute judgment for me. You will bring me out into the light, and I shall behold Your righteousness.

Let not my enemy rejoice over me. Let those who looked upon my pain with pride be silent when they see Your hand upon me. As You have said, "Now shall she be trodden down as the mire of the streets"—so I trust that the enemy who sought to destroy me will be humbled under Your justice. You will make me to tread upon that which once tried to tread upon me.

I surrender to You, my Defender, and I walk forward in the power of Your promise. You are my victory, and in You, I will stand.

In Jesus' name, Amen.

Day 48: Power to Tread

> Behold, I give you authority to tread on serpents and scorpions, and over all the power of the enemy. Nothing will in any way hurt you.
> —Luke 10:19 WEB

Lord Jesus, my Savior and King, I thank You for the authority You have given me. You said, "Behold, I give unto you power to tread on serpents and scorpions, and over all the power of the enemy—and nothing shall by any means hurt you." I receive that promise with a heart full of trust and courage.

No weapon formed against me shall prosper, because I walk in the power of Your name. I do not stand in my own strength, but in the authority You purchased for me with Your blood. I tread upon every lie, every fear, every spiritual attack that rises against me. They are under my feet—not because I am worthy, but because You are victorious.

You have not left me defenseless. You have clothed me with power from on high. The enemy may roar, but he cannot prevail. The serpents may strike, but they cannot wound what You have covered. I stand secure, fearless, and unmoved.

Thank You, Lord, that nothing—nothing—shall by any means hurt me. I walk boldly, not in pride, but in the confidence of Your Word. I am more than a conqueror, because I am Yours.

In Jesus' name, Amen.

Day 49: Crushed Beneath His Feet

> And the God of peace will quickly crush Satan under your feet. The grace of our Lord Jesus Christ be with you.
> —Romans 16:20 WEB

God of peace, my Strong Deliverer, I praise You for the promise that the God of peace shall soon bruise Satan under my feet. What a holy assurance—that the one who has long accused, opposed, and tormented will be crushed beneath the weight of Your victory.

I do not fear the enemy, for his time is short. I do not tremble at his threats, for You have already declared his defeat. You, O Lord, are not only the God of peace, but the God of war—the One who brings peace by overthrowing the works of darkness. And You have chosen to use *my* feet, by Your grace, to tread upon the adversary.

So I stand, not in my own might, but in the grace of Jesus Christ that surrounds me. I wait in faith, knowing that the crushing is coming—that every evil scheme, every demonic stronghold, every whisper of despair will be silenced beneath Your power.

The grace of my Lord Jesus Christ is with me. It strengthens me. It keeps me. It guarantees the final blow. I walk forward in that grace, treading where You've called me to tread, trusting in Your unfailing promise.

In Jesus' name, Amen.

Day 50: The Fall of the Lofty City

> For in this mountain Yahweh's hand will rest. Moab will be trodden down in his place, even like straw is trodden down in the water of the dunghill. He will spread out his hands in the middle of it, like one who swims spreads out hands to swim, but his pride will be humbled together with the craft of his hands. He has brought the high fortress of your walls down, laid low, and brought to the ground, even to the dust.
> —Isaiah 25:10-12 WEB

Lord God, Mighty and Majestic, I praise You for Your hand that rests upon Your people—for on this mountain shall Your hand rest. And Moab, the symbol of pride and opposition, shall be trodden down underfoot, as straw is trampled in the dunghill. You are not silent toward the arrogant. You see every high wall, every fortress of human pride, and You bring it low.

I trust You to bring down every enemy that exalts itself against Your will. Though they spread out their hands in defiance, like a swimmer reaching out to stay afloat, You bring their efforts to nothing. Their walls—the works of their hands, built to defy You—are brought down, laid low, and leveled to the dust.

So I worship You, the One who levels the proud and lifts the humble. I stand upon Your mountain, not by merit, but by mercy. And from this place of peace in Your presence, I tread upon every spiritual enemy that once stood tall. I declare their defeat—not by my might, but by Your outstretched arm.

Your justice is perfect. Your strength is unstoppable. And I will not fear the proud, for You, O Lord, have already declared their end.

In Jesus' name, Amen.

Day 51: Do Valiantly

> Give us help against the enemy, for the help of man is vain. Through God, we will do valiantly. For it is he who will tread down our enemies.
> —Psalms 108:12-13 WEB

O God, my Strength and my Shield, I cry out to You for help—for vain is the help of man. No strategy, no alliance, no earthly power can deliver me like You can. I look to You alone, for You are my sure defense in the face of the enemy.

Through You, we shall do valiantly. It is You who shall tread down our enemies. Not by my own might, not by cleverness or strength, but by Your Spirit, I overcome. You go before me into every battle, and in Your name, the enemy is brought low.

So I will not fear what rises against me. I will not be shaken by threats or intimidated by opposition. For You are with me, and in You, I am victorious. You have made me more than a conqueror, and by Your hand, the enemy is crushed beneath my feet.

Thank You, Lord, that I do not fight alone. You are my Deliverer, and in You, I move forward with courage and praise.

In Jesus' name, Amen.

Day 52: UNDER MY FEET

> You will tread on the lion and cobra. You will trample the young lion and the serpent underfoot.
> —Psalms 91:13 WEB

Most High God, my Refuge and my Fortress, I thank You for the authority You have given me in Your name. You have declared that I shall tread upon the lion and the adder—the fierce and the deceptive—and trample the young lion and the dragon underfoot.

No threat is too great, no enemy too strong, no deception too subtle. In You, I rise in boldness. By Your Spirit, I walk in victory. The powers of darkness may prowl and strike, but they are under my feet because I dwell in the secret place of the Most High and abide under the shadow of the Almighty.

You are with me, and that changes everything. You have not left me vulnerable to the enemy's schemes. You have equipped me to tread, to overcome, to crush what once tried to crush me. Not because I am mighty—but because You are.

So I step forward today without fear. I walk in the victory of the cross. And I declare that every enemy—seen and unseen—is defeated under the authority of Your name.

In Jesus' name, Amen.

Day 53: None Like My God

> You are happy, Israel! Who is like you, a people saved by Yahweh, the shield of your help, the sword of your excellency? Your enemies will submit themselves to you. You will tread on their high places."
> —Deuteronomy 33:29 WEB

Blessed are You, O Lord, my Shield and my Sword, the One who saves me and calls me Your own. Truly, I am blessed as Your child—there is none like You, the God who rides the heavens to help me, who moves in majesty and might on my behalf.

You are my refuge, my dwelling place, and underneath are the everlasting arms. You drive out my enemies before me and command their destruction—not by my strength, but by Your decree. I shout in victory, not because of what I've done, but because of who You are.

The enemy rises, but You bring him low. He plots, but You scatter his plans. You trample down every force that stands against Your purpose in my life, and You place my feet in the land of promise.

O Lord, my King and my Defender, I rejoice in Your salvation. I live in safety because of You. And I tread upon the enemy with confidence, knowing that it is You who fights for me.

In Jesus' name, Amen.

Day 54: SUREFOOTED VICTORY

> Yahweh, the Lord, is my strength. He makes my feet like deer's feet, and enables me to go in high places. For the music director, on my stringed instruments.
> —Habakkuk 3:19 WEB

Lord God, my Strength and my Sustainer, I praise You—for You make my feet like hinds' feet, and You cause me to walk upon my high places. When the path is steep and the climb is hard, You steady me. When the ground beneath me shakes, You lift me up above the storm.

You are not only my refuge—you are the One who gives me strength to move forward. You make me swift and sure, even in battle. You train my steps for victory, and You cause me to rise above every enemy, every obstacle, every fear.

When I feel weak, You remind me: You are my strength. When I feel surrounded, You lift me to higher ground. In You, I do not sink—I stand. I do not stumble—I climb. You place me above the threat and teach me to tread upon the heights.

Thank You, Lord, for making me strong in You. I walk boldly in the places where the enemy once tried to keep me bound. You are faithful, and You are my song.

In Jesus' name, Amen.

Day 55: Feet on Their Necks

> When they brought those kings out to Joshua, Joshua called for all the men of Israel, and said to the chiefs of the men of war who went with him, "Come near. Put your feet on the necks of these kings." They came near, and put their feet on their necks. Joshua said to them, "Don't be afraid, nor be dismayed. Be strong and courageous, for Yahweh will do this to all your enemies against whom you fight."
> —Joshua 10:24-25 WEB

Lord God, Mighty Warrior and Commander of Heaven's Armies, I thank You for the victory You give to those who trust in You. Just as Joshua called the leaders of Israel to place their feet on the necks of their enemies, so I stand today in the authority of Your name, treading upon every force that rises against Your purpose in my life.

You have said, "Fear not, nor be dismayed, be strong and of good courage," and I receive that word deep in my spirit. I will not tremble at the size of the enemy or the strength of their weapons. For You, O Lord, fight for me. You deliver every adversary into my hands—not by might, nor by power, but by Your Spirit.

Let every spiritual enemy that once stood tall now be brought low. Let every chain be crushed underfoot. You have made me more than a conqueror, and I walk in boldness—not in pride, but in the confidence of Your covenant.

You are the God who fights for Your people, and in You, I will not be moved.

In Jesus' name, Amen.

Day 56: Sit at My Right Hand

A Psalm by David. Yahweh says to my Lord, "Sit at my right hand, until I make your enemies your footstool for your feet."
—Psalms 110:1 WEB

Lord God, my Sovereign and King, I exalt You for the power and majesty of Your throne. You have said to my Lord, "Sit Thou at My right hand, until I make Thine enemies Thy footstool." What comfort and strength that brings to my soul—knowing that every enemy is being placed beneath the feet of Christ, who reigns forever.

You are not anxious over evil. You are enthroned above it. And because I belong to Jesus, I share in His victory. The enemies that war against my soul, the darkness that threatens to overwhelm—You are making them His footstool. They will bow. They will fall. They will be silenced beneath His rule.

So I wait with confidence. I do not fight for victory—I fight from it. I am seated with Christ in heavenly places, and I know that the outcome is secure. You are faithful to fulfill Your Word. You will bring every opposition into submission under His feet.

And until that day is complete, I will worship, I will trust, and I will stand firm in the triumph of my King.

In Jesus' name, Amen.

Day 57: Until All Enemies Fall

> For he must reign until he has put all his enemies under his feet. For, "He put all things in subjection under his feet." But when he says, "All things are put in subjection", it is evident that he is excepted who subjected all things to him.
> —1 Corinthians 15:25, 27 WEB

Lord Jesus, Risen King and Eternal Victor, I worship You—because You must reign until all enemies are put under Your feet. And God has put all things in subjection under You. Nothing is beyond Your rule, nothing escapes Your authority, and no enemy will stand forever.

I rest in this holy truth: You are reigning now. Even as the battle rages and darkness resists, You are not moved. You are conquering every enemy—every fear, every sin, every power of death and hell. You are bringing all things into submission, until the last enemy is crushed beneath Your feet.

And because I am in You, I share in that triumph. I no longer live in defeat, for You are my victory. I walk in hope, knowing that every enemy still present is already destined to fall. You are reigning in my life, and I surrender to Your authority with joy and trust.

Finish Your work in me, Lord. Reign in every corner of my heart. Let nothing rise above You—and let every enemy that tries to remain be brought low by the power of Your name.

In Jesus' name, Amen.

Day 58: THE FALL OF THE PROUD

> Look at everyone who is proud, and humble him. Crush the wicked in their place.
> —Job 40:12 WEB

Almighty God, the One who sees the proud from afar and humbles them with a breath, I honor Your holiness and bow before Your justice. You look on every one that is proud and bring them low. You tread down the wicked where they stand, no matter how high they lift themselves in arrogance.

You are the Judge of all the earth, and no evil escapes Your eye. While the proud exalt themselves in strength, You scatter them with a word. You bring down the lofty and expose the hidden. You crush the rebellion of the wicked—not out of cruelty, but to establish righteousness and truth.

So I trust You, Lord, in every battle. I do not need to fight in my own strength or answer every insult. I know that You are the One who humbles the enemy. I leave room for Your justice, and I find peace in the power of Your hand.

Tread down, O God, every wicked plan that rises against Your will in my life. Let the proud fall, and let Your name be exalted.

In Jesus' name, Amen.

Day 59: Treading the Lofty Down

> For he has brought down those who dwell on high, the lofty city. He lays it low. He lays it low even to the ground. He brings it even to the dust. The foot shall tread it down; Even the feet of the poor, and the steps of the needy."
> —Isaiah 26:5-6 WEB

Most High God, You are the One who humbles the proud and exalts the lowly. You have brought down the lofty city—You lay it low, even to the ground; You cast it to the dust. And the feet of the poor, the steps of the needy, shall tread it down.

I praise You, Lord, for being the God who sees the oppressed and lifts them up. You do not ignore the cries of the broken. You overthrow the proud and make a way for the humble to walk in victory. What once towered over me, You have brought low. What once seemed unshakable, You have crushed beneath the power of Your justice.

So I will not fear strongholds or high places. I will trust in You, my Deliverer. You make a path where there was none. You cause me to tread in places I once thought impossible to reach. The very ground where I was once trampled, You now give me to walk in freedom.

Thank You, Lord, for exalting the weak and shattering the prideful. I walk forward in hope and courage, because You go before me.

In Jesus' name, Amen.

Day 60: Ashes Under My Feet

> You shall tread down the wicked; for they will be ashes under the soles of your feet in the day that I make," says Yahweh of Armies.
>
> —Malachi 4:3 WEB

Lord of Hosts, Righteous and Faithful, I thank You for the promise of Your justice. You have declared that the day will come when the righteous shall tread down the wicked—for they shall be ashes under the soles of our feet, in the day that You act.

I do not walk in vengeance, Lord, but in the assurance that You are a God who makes all things right. You see every act of evil, every hand lifted against Your truth, and You have appointed a day when the proud and the wicked will be no more. Their strength will turn to dust, and their threats will vanish like smoke.

You have called me to walk in righteousness, not in fear. To stand in holiness, not in hate. And because I belong to You, I will see the triumph of light over darkness. You will make the enemy's end a testimony to Your glory and a path for Your people to walk forward in peace.

Let me walk humbly, yet boldly. Let me never forget that my victory is not in myself, but in You. You are the God who acts, and in You, I stand secure.

In Jesus' name, Amen.

Day 61: LIKE A LION AMONG FLOCKS

> The remnant of Jacob will be among the nations, among many peoples, like a lion among the animals of the forest, like a young lion among the flocks of sheep; who, if he goes through, treads down and tears in pieces, and there is no one to deliver. Let your hand be lifted up above your adversaries, and let all of your enemies be cut off.
> —Micah 5:8-9 WEB

Lord God, Mighty in the midst of Your people, I thank You that You have made me as a lion among the nations—strong not in myself, but in You. As a lion among the beasts of the forest, as a young lion among flocks of sheep, so You have positioned Your remnant: fearless, bold, and victorious through Your Spirit.

I do not tremble before the enemy. By Your power, I rise above intimidation and stand firm in the authority You have given. When I go forth in Your name, none can deliver out of my hand, for it is not my hand, but Yours at work within me.

Let my hand be lifted up over my adversaries, Lord, and let all my enemies be cut off—not by sword or strength, but by Your divine hand. You are the One who delivers, who defends, and who gives dominion to those who walk in Your fear.

So I rest in this truth: I am not abandoned. I am not powerless. I am a child of the King, and You have made me to overcome. Let all who oppose Your will see Your strength rise in me—and let Your name be glorified in every victory.

In Jesus' name, Amen.

Day 62: Dust Beneath My Feet

> Then I beat them as small as the dust of the earth. I crushed them as the mire of the streets, and spread them abroad.
> —2 Samuel 22:43 WEB

Lord, my Deliverer and Avenger, I praise You for the power of Your hand that brings justice and triumph. You have made my enemies as the dust of the earth—crushed beneath Your feet, scattered by the breath of Your Spirit. As the mire of the streets, You have beaten them small and cast them away.

I do not boast in my own strength, for it is You who fights for me. You rise up on my behalf and shatter every force that stands in opposition to Your purpose in my life. The enemy that once threatened me now lies broken, not because of who I am, but because of who You are.

You are the God who redeems, who restores, and who rules with righteousness. I trust You to continue the work You've begun—to silence the accuser, to tear down the strongholds, and to establish me in the place of victory.

Let my heart stay humble and my hands clean, for the battle belongs to You. I walk in freedom today because You have crushed what once tried to crush me.

In Jesus' name, Amen.

Day 63: WAR HORSES OF THE LORD

> They shall be as mighty men, treading down muddy streets in the battle; and they shall fight, because Yahweh is with them; and the riders on horses will be confounded.
> —Zechariah 10:5 WEB

Lord God of Heaven's Armies, I praise You for making Your people like mighty warriors—like horses prepared for battle. You have promised that we shall be as mighty men, who tread down our enemies in the mire of the streets in battle. You, O Lord, go with us, and because of You, we overcome.

I do not stand in fear, for You have trained my hands for war and strengthened my heart for the fight. You are not distant from the struggle—You are in the midst of it. You make me bold like a lion, swift like a stallion, steady like a soldier who knows the victory is already assured.

Because You are with me, I will not retreat. Because You are faithful, I will not fall. My enemies may surround me, but they are no match for the One who fights beside me. I tread upon them, not in pride, but in the confidence of Your covenant promise.

Thank You, Lord, for making me strong through Your presence and sure through Your Word. Let every enemy be brought low, and let Your name be exalted in every triumph.

In Jesus' name, Amen.

Day 64: THE WINEPRESS OF JUSTICE

> "I have trodden the wine press alone; and of the peoples, no one was with me: Yes, I trod them in my anger, and trampled them in my wrath. Their lifeblood is sprinkled on my garments, and I have stained all my clothing. For the day of vengeance was in my heart, and the year of my redeemed has come. I trod down the peoples in my anger, and made them drunk in my wrath, and I poured out their lifeblood on the earth."
> —Isaiah 63: 3-4, 6 WEB

Lord, Mighty and Just, I stand in awe of Your power and righteousness. You have declared that You alone have trodden the winepress, and of the people there was none with You. In Your fury, You have crushed the nations; in Your wrath, You have trampled them down, and their lifeblood is sprinkled upon Your garments. This is not the rage of man—but the holy judgment of the Lord against all evil.

You looked, and it was the day of vengeance in Your heart. You saw the suffering of Your people, and the year of Your redeemed had come. You rose, not in silence, but with zeal. You brought justice where there was oppression. You poured out wrath where there was rebellion.

And now, Lord, I take refuge in Your justice. I trust in Your power to trample every enemy underfoot—not only those who stand against me, but all who defy Your name. You have made it known that no evil will escape Your judgment, and no darkness will go unchallenged by Your light.

Thank You for being a God who acts. Thank You for standing up for the afflicted and redeeming those who trust in You. I surrender to Your justice, and I walk in the confidence of Your final victory.

In Jesus' name, Amen.

PART 5: WHEN HEAVEN STRIKES

There are moments in spiritual warfare when God does not simply defend—He invades. He rides upon the storm. He thunders from His throne. He releases lightning, arrows, and fear into the camp of the enemy. When heaven strikes, it is not subtle—it is unmistakable. It is the holy interruption of God into the affairs of men and devils alike.

In this section, we pray from the place of awe and authority, calling on the Lord of Hosts to stretch forth His hand in power. These are not gentle prayers; they are war cries. We ask God to scatter, strike, shake, and rescue. We agree with heaven's judgment upon evil, trusting the God who saves with fire and delivers with force.

When heaven strikes, the proud fall, the wicked flee, and the righteous rise in strength. This is not our vengeance—it is God's justice. And when He moves, nothing can stand in His way.

Day 65: Who Can Stand?

> The mountains quake before him, and the hills melt away. The earth trembles at his presence, yes, the world, and all who dwell in it. Who can stand before his indignation? Who can endure the fierceness of his anger? His wrath is poured out like fire, and the rocks are broken apart by him.
> —Nahum 1:5-6 WEB

Lord God Almighty, the earth trembles before You. The mountains quake, the hills melt, and no force of man or darkness can remain standing when You arise in Your wrath. Who can stand before Your indignation? Who can endure the fire of Your fury? You are not indifferent to evil. You are not silent in the face of injustice. You move in righteous judgment to tear down the works of the enemy and avenge Your name.

When I feel overwhelmed by powers too great for me, I remember that nothing and no one is greater than You. You are not afraid of the proud. You are not intimidated by armies. You are not shaken by threats. You are the One who speaks, and the whole earth responds. And I belong to You.

So I trust You, Lord, to fight for me. I trust You to move against every spirit, every lie, every scheme that rises against me. Let every high thing be brought low before You. Let every evil work melt like wax in the fire of Your presence. Bring down strongholds that I cannot touch, and cause Your righteousness to blaze like the sun.

In reverent fear and steadfast faith, I wait for You to act. For I know when You rise, no enemy will remain.

In Jesus' name, Amen.

Day 66: They Shall Be as Nothing

> Behold, all those who are incensed against you will be disappointed and confounded. Those who strive with you will be like nothing, and shall perish. You will seek them, and won't find them, even those who contend with you. Those who war against you will be as nothing, as a non-existent thing.
> —Isaiah 41:11-12 WEB

Holy God, my Shield and Defender, I thank You that those who rise up against me do not have the final word. You see every enemy—every accuser, every oppressor, every spiritual force that seeks my downfall—and You have declared that they shall be ashamed and confounded. Their threats will collapse. Their plans will scatter. Their strength will fade into nothing.

I will not fear those who strive with me. I will not be dismayed by the war around me. For You are with me. You uphold me with Your righteous right hand. You silence those who mock, and You disarm those who attack. You turn back the weapons of the enemy and bring confusion to their camp.

You promise that I will seek them and not find them. I will look for those who tormented me—and they will be gone, like a shadow fleeing the sunrise. Lord, make it so. In every place the enemy has roared against me, let Your voice thunder louder. In every place I have felt surrounded, let Your presence draw near and make my enemies vanish like smoke in the wind.

Thank You, Father, that You never leave Your children defenseless. You fight with power, and You win with mercy. I stand firm, because You are near.

In Jesus' name, Amen.

Day 67: Delivered from the Strong

> He delivered me from my strong enemy, from those who hated me; for they were too mighty for me.
> —Psalms 18:17 WEB

Faithful Deliverer, I worship You. You have reached into battles where I was overwhelmed and pulled me out from the grip of enemies too strong for me. I have felt crushed, cornered, and outnumbered—but You were not. What overpowered me could not overpower You. What hated me could not resist Your love.

The enemy came with weapons, but You came with glory. The enemy came with chains, but You broke through with light. You are the One who rescues me from battles I cannot win and lifts me out of pits too deep for my strength. You saw me in my weakness and still chose to fight for me.

I acknowledge today that I need You. I surrender my attempts to save myself. I lay down the fear that tells me I'm alone. I am not alone. I have a Deliverer. And You are greater than the darkness. Let Your hand be strong for me again. Rescue me from every voice of accusation, every snare of temptation, every force that hates what You are doing in my life.

You are not late. You are not weary. You are the God who delivers from the strong.

In Jesus' name, Amen.

Day 68: BROUGHT DOWN FROM THE HEIGHTS

> The pride of your heart has deceived you, you who dwell in the clefts of the rock, whose habitation is high, who says in his heart, 'Who will bring me down to the ground?' Though you mount on high as the eagle, and though your nest is set among the stars, I will bring you down from there," says Yahweh.
> —Obadiah 1:3-4 WEB

Sovereign Lord, You see through the pride of the wicked. You are not deceived by their appearance or impressed by their height. Though they exalt themselves like the eagle, though they build their nests in the stars, You bring them down. No fortress can protect them from Your judgment. No strategy can outwit Your justice.

You know the heart, and You will not let the proud go unchallenged. When the arrogant speak boastfully, You will answer with thunder. When they stretch out their hand against the righteous, You will stretch out Yours with power. I praise You, Lord, for being the God who humbles the proud and exalts the lowly.

Let every high place that exalts itself against Your knowledge be torn down. Let the proud who defy Your name be brought to nothing. And keep me, Lord, from the pride that blinds. Keep me low before You, walking humbly, depending daily on Your mercy. I do not trust in myself—I trust in You.

You alone are worthy to be lifted high. Let all who oppose You fall, and let Your glory rise.

In Jesus' name, Amen.

Day 69: He Shall Prevail

> Yahweh will go out like a mighty man. He will stir up zeal like a man of war. He will raise a war cry. Yes, he will shout aloud. He will triumph over his enemies.
> —Isaiah 42:13 WEB

Mighty God, Man of War, rise up and fight on behalf of Your people. You are not passive. You are not silent. You go forth like a mighty man, roaring in holy zeal. You stir Yourself in battle, and You prevail against all Your enemies.

I call on You now, Lord—make war in the heavens on my behalf. Let every demonic force, every stronghold, every entrenched lie be struck down by Your voice. Let every spiritual enemy that seeks to destroy my peace be silenced by the sound of Your cry. You are not only the Lamb who saves, You are the Lion who conquers.

Go before me and break through the barriers. Roar over my home, my mind, and my life. Prevail in the places I cannot see. Fight for the weary. Defend the defenseless. And let every knee bow to the name of Jesus.

I will not retreat. I will not panic. I trust in the One who fights for me. You have never lost a battle—and You never will.

In Jesus' name, Amen.

Day 70: LIGHTNING AND DELIVERANCE

> Throw out lightning, and scatter them. Send out your arrows, and rout them. Stretch out your hand from above, rescue me, and deliver me out of great waters, out of the hands of foreigners;
> —Psalms 144:6-7 WEB

O Lord my Rock, stretch forth Your hand and deliver me. Cast forth lightning from Your throne—scatter the forces of darkness. Shoot out Your arrows and send the enemy running. Let Your power descend like fire and drive back every threat that surrounds me.

You are the God who parts the heavens. You are the One who reaches down to rescue. From the deep waters of affliction, You lift me. From the snares of the wicked, You set me free. No weapon formed against me can stand when You rise.

Rescue me, Lord, not only from what others do—but from what lurks within: from fear, from despair, from doubt. Break every chain. Silence every voice of the accuser. Let the enemies of my soul be scattered before You like smoke before the wind.

I praise You, Lord, not just for what You do—but for who You are: my Deliverer, my Fortress, my Mighty One. Stretch forth Your hand again, and I will praise You with all my strength.

In Jesus' name, Amen.

Epilogue

You've made it through 70 days of warfare prayer—and something has shifted. Perhaps it's the way you speak now. Or the way you see. Or the way you stand when opposition comes. You're not who you were when you began this journey.

But know this: the battle isn't over, and the enemy doesn't rest. Yet neither does your God. He who neither slumbers nor sleeps watches over you with fire in His eyes and victory in His hands. You are not fighting for victory—you are fighting from it.

Keep praying. Keep declaring. Keep treading. Let the enemy find you unafraid, fully armed, and deeply rooted in the Word. Let your voice be a war cry that reminds darkness it cannot win.

You are not alone in this fight. Heaven is with you. The Lord of Hosts goes before you. And the victory is still His.

Now rise—and engage.

In Jesus' name, Amen.

Encourage Others with Your Story

If this book has encouraged or strengthened you in your journey toward deliverance, I would be grateful if you could share your experience by leaving a review on Amazon. Your honest feedback not only helps me grow but also encourages others seeking God's protection and peace to find hope through these prayers and Scriptures.

Thank you for letting this book be part of your walk with God. May His deliverance continue to surround you every day!

More from PrayerScripts

SCRIPTURES & PRAYERS FOR DELIVERANCE FROM TROUBLE: 40 DAYS OF PRAYER FOR WHEN LIFE FEELS OVERWHELMING

Are you walking through a season where life feels heavy, hope feels distant, and your prayers feel weak?

Scriptures & Prayers for Deliverance from Trouble is a 40-day journey of honest prayers and powerful Scriptures to help you find peace, strength, and healing when life is overwhelming. Each day offers a personal, Scripture-based prayer written in the language of real faith and raw trust. This devotional isn't about perfect words—it's about real connection with God when you need Him most.

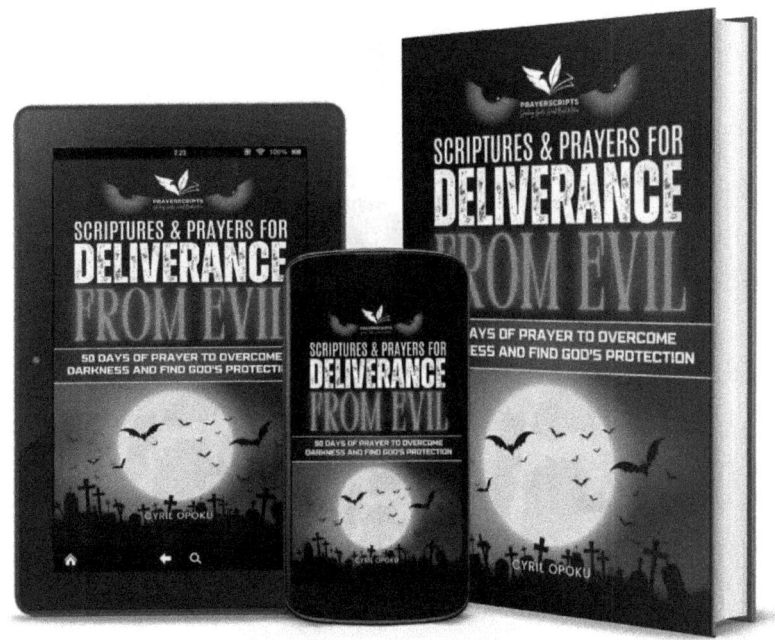

SCRIPTURES & PRAYERS FOR DELIVERANCE FROM EVIL:
50 DAYS OF PRAYER TO OVERCOME DARKNESS AND FIND GOD'S PROTECTION

When darkness presses in, how do you pray?

When fear grips your heart or unseen battles rage around you, you need more than generic words—you need Scripture, truth, and the steady hand of God to lead you through.

Scriptures & Prayers for Deliverance from Evil: 50 Days of Prayer to Overcome Darkness and Find God's Protection is a powerful devotional journey designed to help you pray boldly and biblically through seasons of spiritual warfare, oppression, fear, or uncertainty.

<u>Scriptures & Prayers for Combating Spiritual Wickedness:</u>
<u>50 Days of Prayer to Overthrow Wicked Plans and Stand in God's Victory</u>

Are you facing opposition that feels deeper than the natural? Do you sense hidden resistance working against your progress, peace, or purpose? You're not imagining it—and you're not powerless.

Rooted in the authority of Scripture and fueled by bold, targeted prayers, *Scriptures & Prayers for Combating Spiritual Wickedness* equips you to confront darkness head-on. Each day features a focused Bible passage and a heartfelt, Scripture-based prayer designed to nullify ungodly counsel, disrupt demonic schemes, and establish God's victory in every area of your life.

www.ingramcontent.com/pod-product-compliance
Lightning Source LLC
Chambersburg PA
CBHW060405050426
42449CB00009B/1907